T0273644

empowerment.

the portable companion for girls, young women, and the modern woman

empowerment.

the portable companion for girls, young women, and the modern woman

Dedicated To My Daughter Maya

I composed 'empowerment' to educate my 8-year-old daughter Maya on the limitless possibilities of what she can achieve when she becomes a woman. For one year I wrote an affirmation every morning to read to her as she awoke for the school day. Positive statements to empower her to find inner strength, overcome self-doubts, and encourage self-esteem and value. My hope is for every girl or young woman who encounters this book, to believe in themselves, that they can achieve anything they set their minds to. To wholeheartedly focus on manifesting their dreams and aspirations instead of dependency and the perception of being the inferior and or weaker sex. To never be influenced by negative people's thoughts and opinions.

empowerment.

the portable companion for girls, young women, and the modern woman

Always remember you are the sum of your thoughts.

If you think, or believe you won't win, you will lose.

If you believe you're not good enough, you've convinced yourself you're not.

A quitter will never succeed.

Never give into doubt, fear, or weakness.

To achieve your goals, you must have a plan then execute.

In life you will encounter obstacles that require navigation through the power of thought process.

Life is a steady stream of interactions between the conscious and unconscious.

Not every problem has a logical answer.

You can only be a boss if you put in the work.

Never be too concerned with the thoughts, opinions, and actions of others.

You can't control anyone but your own behavior, thoughts, and words.

Every human being is born with a purpose. To accomplish their mission in this lifetime is entirely up to them.

Always focus on yourself and block out all fear, doubt, and negativity.

Distractions are counterproductive and keep you from achieving a higher level of enlightenment.

Life is to be taken seriously. It's not a joke, and it's not easy. It's simple and completely complicated. If you're not careful, everyday will be a constant struggle, unrelenting and unforgivable.

In life, you will need a strategy to be victorious.

You must always keep your eye on the prize.

You will achieve all you want in this life if you make the right decisions and learn from your mistakes.

You must be prepared for life's obstacles, the seen and unseen.

If you work hard, and with a little luck your dreams will become your reality.

Always strive to overachieve in your studies, for this is the key element to forecast your future.

You will not be perfect and fail some test, but always revisit what you answered incorrectly, so you don't repeat the mistakes.

Never believe someone loves you if they are not showing you their love. It's not enough to say the words but you must feel loved. Never forget this because it will save you a tremendous amount of heartache.

Always look for the signs on the journey to guide you to your destination. No matter how dire a moment or situation may appear, you are exactly where you're supposed to be.

A test reveals what we have learned and where we need to refocus.

Never be scared to be tested. The only person who fears a test is the one who is not prepared.

Life is a process, essential for you to manifest destiny.

The World is equal parts ugly and beautiful.

In Life there is a constant struggle regarding good versus evil.

Weak people will attempt to convince you they are stronger than you. It's strategic, not to respond with ego but with tact.

Pretending to be weak when you're strong and strong when you're weak will always give you the advantage over your opponent. It will lure them into a false sense of security which is a façade.

Overconfidence could be detrimental to your downfall.

Always expect the unexpected.

Never talk about who you are, let your actions show the World who you are.

Close your eyes and imagine yourself living the life you want. If you can see it, you can be it.

Never look away when faced with defeat. Never give in to losing if you haven't already lost. Summon the fight left in you. Believe you will overcome defeat and you will stand victorious.

I'm so fortunate and blessed to have you as my daughter.

You give my life purpose and meaning.

Never forget to be thankful for what you have, not what you don't have.

Fill your life with an abundance of laughter, kindness, and generosity.

You are my love, my life, my daughter.

You are a strong, beautiful, smart, loving, generous, kind, and honest.

Realize your true and vast potential.

People are like plants, and flowers, how you care for them matters. Your words and actions will either give them life or cause their demise.

Be careful who you offend and who attempts to offend you.

Never be defined by what others think of you.

Hurt people, will always hurt people because it's their defense mechanism.

I believe without any question of doubt, you will
change the World for the better.

You are an old soul, knowledgeable beyond your years.

I'm so happy you picked me to be your father.

You are the best and worst of me, and you are loved.

Never put off for tomorrow what can be accomplished today.

You are the pride of our ancestors and their dreams manifested.

Always stay true to you and who you are and how you want to be perceived in the World.

Loving you, and being loved by you, unconditionally is the greatest gift I have ever given and received.

To be a great leader, you first must be a great listener.

Take your time and never rush to judgment.

Respect elders who are wise, experienced, and can teach you valuable lessons in life.

You are the only person you can trust 100%. Always listen to your inner voice and your gut. Never go against your intuitive, and instinctual voice.

Communication is the key to an amicable result.

Make decisions based on rationality and logic, never emotions.

Never diagnose someone by their symptoms alone. Examine the root of the problem as the cause of the symptoms and dispense prescription accordingly.

Life is a marathon, not a race.

Every moment, decision, defines your life.

Look deep inside your soul for the answers to the tough questions. Never allow yourself to be manipulated and or coerced into believing what is irrational and analogical.

Care for the health and well-being of others,
especially those you love.

Never assume you know everything.

Take your time, access the problem, set the equation, and apply the solution.

I'm your Dad, I want to educate and inform you to set the precedent. I will teach you essential life lessons allowing you a chance to live your best life.

It's OK not to know everything but it's not OK not to try.

You are born alone, and you will die, alone.

The in-between time you spend in search for your true self will define you.

You are the best version of me.

Anything and everything in moderation.

Love your life, live to love and love to live.

Life is filled with uncertainty, but you must trust your instincts.

Take one step at a time and never lose sight of what's in front of you.

Take your time in hopes of doing it correctly the first time.

It's important to know your past but don't live in the past, live for today, and prepare for tomorrow.

You must forgive all those who hurt you and meant you harm. You cannot harbor anger or wish them ill will because we are all connected.

Communication, organization, are two keys to success.

Stay focused and stay in your lane.

People change. Their change doesn't mean they are not who they were. It only means they have changed. We can still love them for the moments we shared and the memories, but we must move on before the language becomes disdainful, hurtful, and disrespectful.

I'm so proud of your imperfections.

We are on this Earth to experience. Each person has a unique dynamic. In the end you will not be judged.

No fear of the unknown.

You are my heart. Everything I do is for you. No one means more to me than you.

Power of thought and mind over matter are essential to physical, emotional, and mental well-being.

You must know when to embrace change.

Listen to your inner voice.

Your laughter is glorious, harmonious, and infectious. It's a constant reminder how happiness, love, and care lives inside of you.

The World is your playground but if you're not careful could turn into your prison.

Don't be concerned with the words, thoughts, and actions of others unless it directly and or indirectly affects you.

Stay the course and the universe will guide you to your destination.

Girls are as strong or stronger than boys. Never believe you are the weaker sex.

You and I have known each other since the beginning of time. When this life comes to an end we will find each other again, and again in perpetuity.

For those who do not attempt to better themselves and strive for a better quality of life will be haunted and plagued by the thought of what if.

Always be a person of your word because your reputation is paramount.

Never lie or be dishonest unless it's a matter of living a better quality of life or death.

Your word is your currency.

Be a person that can be trusted, respected, and has significant value.

Always see the beauty in everything and everyone.

Never judge people by their education, or appearance.

Judge people by their character, actions, and words.

Your health is more important than anything in your life.

Without health, you have nothing.

Always remember to take very good care of yourself.

Your future is in full view for all to see.

Never settle for less, and always strive for excellence.

You get out what you put in. Always 110%.

Always dream, but there is no dream without passion, and commitment.

You are young, gifted, and talented.

There are no third chances for anyone that has lied or deceived you.

Your friendship should be earned and rewarded.

Always tell the truth no matter the consequences.

Never want to be anyone but you.

You are on this planet for a purpose.

Believe you can, and you will. See yourself where you want to be, and you will be.

Never let anyone have power over you.

Stand with the power of truth and you will never be defeated.

This World is not fair.

There are people who can only communicate in conflict, and they should be avoided at all costs.

You are a champion.

You are defined by your decisions.

You are the definition of humanity.

Never be afraid of the unknown.

We must overcome our fears and embrace our phobias.

Your health is paramount; your body is a temple.

This is the start of a new week to work on being the
best of who you are destined to be.

Push yourself, know no limits.

One day you will reap the fruit of your commitment, dedication, and hard work.

Always be inspired to be a better person.

We all start from the beginning; we strive for the middle and finish hard.

For some, there is only one chance, one choice.

You are the prettier, smarter, younger, and stronger version of your Papa.

Never pick anyone over your studies, or family.

Life is by design.

Not everyone will play by the rules.

Just because someone is in your family doesn't mean they are nice, loving, kind or should be trusted.

Make sure you're comfortable with the end-result before you walk away.

Work smarter, not harder and everything in life is attainable.

I wish I could live forever to share this journey of life with you.